D1710067

DISCARD

Careers in Law Enforcement

ReferencePoint Press®

Other titles in the *Exploring Careers* series include:

Careers in Law Enforcement

Michael V. Uschan

ReferencePoint
Press®

For more information, contact:
ReferencePoint Press, Inc.
PO Box 27779
San Diego, CA 92198
www.ReferencePointPress.com

LIBRARY OF CONGRESS CATALOGING-IN-PUBLICATION DATA

Names: Uschan, Michael V., 1948– author.
Title: Careers in law enforcement / by Michael V. Uschan.
Description: San Diego, CA : ReferencePoint Press, [2017] | Series: Exploring careers | Audience:
    Grade 9 to 12. | Includes bibliographical references and index.
Identifiers: LCCN 2016033015 (print) | LCCN 2016048683 (ebook) | ISBN 9781682821060
    (hardback) | ISBN 9781682821077 (eBook)
Subjects: LCSH: Law enforcement--Vocational guidance--United States--Juvenile literature. |
    Police--Vocational guidance--United States--Juvenile literature.
Classification: LCC HV8143 .U83 2017 (print) | LCC HV8143 (ebook) | DDC 363.2023/73--dc23
LC record available at https://lccn.loc.gov/2016033015

Contents

Working in Law Enforcement

S tudents were leaving the Antigo (Wisconsin) High School prom around eleven o'clock in the evening of April 23, 2016, when the unthinkable happened—someone began shooting at them. Two teenagers were injured before Patrolman Andy Hopfensperger shot and killed the assailant. Hopfensperger and a second officer had been monitoring cars leaving the school parking lot as the prom ended. But when the shooting began, Hopfensperger immediately began performing the most important role of a police officer—protecting citizens from being harmed. In a *Milwaukee Journal-Sentinel* story two days later, the family of one of the wounded students thanked Hopfensperger for saving "the lives of our son, their two friends, and the countless amount of students, staff and others in and around the school."

Hopfensperger was performing the essential task of all law enforcement officers, which is "to protect and serve" the public. The Los Angeles Police Department adopted that motto in 1955 to define the daily mission of its police officers. The motto refers to protecting the lives and property of citizens and serving them in many other ways. It has been widely accepted as the definitive statement of what all law enforcement officers do.

Police officers like Hopfensperger are the most familiar face of law enforcement to the public because they are the most visible. People in communities across the nation see them daily, walking or driving through their neighborhoods, issuing traffic citations, responding to emergencies and reports of crimes, and making arrests. Police officers, however, represent only one area of law enforcement. There are many others. On its website, the Bureau of Justice Statistics states, "Law enforcement describes the individuals and agencies responsible for enforcing laws and maintaining public order and public safety. Law enforcement includes the prevention, detection, and investigation of crime, and the apprehension and detention of individuals suspected of law violation."

Many Types of Careers

Law enforcement is a diverse field, with jobs at various levels of government. Crime scene investigators, for instance, use scientific methods to collect and examine evidence in criminal cases. Animal control officers are responsible for ensuring the welfare of animals, especially in their interactions with people. Cybersecurity analysts use technology to thwart cybercrime and cyberterrorism. Probation officers monitor the activities of individuals convicted of crimes when they are released from jail or prison, to help them stay out of trouble. Medical examiners perform autopsies on the bodies of people to determine if they died from natural causes or if they were murdered. Arson investigators examine fire scenes and collect evidence to discover if fires were accidental or set on purpose. Game warden is another law enforcement job. Kyle Hladick chose to become a game warden because he enjoyed outdoor activities like hunting, fishing, and hiking in wilderness areas. On the Maine game warden's website, Hladick explains his thinking: "I feel honored to be able to serve in a job which enables me to help preserve the outdoor heritage and natural resources that have had such a significant impact on my own life."

Future Jobs

There are more than 1 million law enforcement personnel at all levels of local, state, and federal government. Although their mission is the same—to protect people, solve crimes, and capture criminals— the scope of their job and how they do it can be quite different. For example, local law enforcement officers may focus on stopping sales of illegal drugs by arresting individual dealers who sell them directly to customers. But federal law enforcement officials like agents for the Drug Enforcement Administration have a much broader goal in the nation's war on drugs; they work at shutting down the overall

Careers in Law Enforcement

Occupation	Entry-level education	2015 median pay
Animal Control Worker	High school diploma or equivalent	$35,330
Bailiff	High school diploma or equivalent	$44,900
Correctional Officer and Jailer	High school diploma or equivalent	$45,320
Detective and Criminal Investigator	High school diploma	$79,620
Emergency Dispatcher	High school diploma or equivalent	$38,010
Fire Inspector	High school diploma or equivalent	$54,790
Forensic Science Technician	Bachelor's degree	$56,320
Game Warden	High school diploma or equivalent	$52,780
Judge and Hearing Officer	Bachelor's, Master's, or Doctoral degree	$109,010
Police and Sheriff Patrol	High school diploma	$60,270
Probation Officer/ Correctional Treatment Specialist	Bachelor's degree	$49,360
Security Guard and Gaming Surveillance	High school diploma or equivalent	$24,680

Bureau of Labor Statistics, *Occupational Outlook Handbook*. www.bls.gov/ooh.

movement of illegal drugs into the nation and between cities and states. Instead of arresting someone selling marijuana or cocaine on a street corner, their goal is to arrest high-level gang leaders who control drug trafficking.

Law enforcement officers at local, state, and federal levels of government cooperate in enforcing the nation's laws. For example, the FBI may work with local police to solve murders and other serious crimes. But state and federal agencies have jurisdiction over certain types of crimes. The FBI, for example, has the major responsibility for enforcing laws and investigating crimes involving more than one state, such as moving women across state lines for the purpose of prostitution. It also plays a lead role in crimes concerning corruption of government officials and kidnapping.

The Bureau of Labor Statistics (BLS) predicts most law enforcement jobs at all levels will increase by 3 percent to 4 percent through 2024, which is below the average of 6.5 percent for all jobs. However, some jobs—including crime scene investigators and animal control officers—will probably experience faster growth than that. The BLS predicts crime scene investigator jobs will increase by 27 percent and animal control officer jobs by 11 percent through 2024. The hiring outlook for members of minority groups and women is also slightly better for law enforcement jobs because many agencies are trying to increase the diversity of their workforces. Additionally, because law enforcement jobs tend to be stressful and can be dangerous, early retirement is not uncommon. This creates more job opportunities for people pursuing such work.

Police Officer

What Do Police Officers Do?

Charles H. Ramsey led both the District of Columbia and Philadelphia police departments. In a commentary on the National Criminal Justice Reference Service website, Ramsey defined the work police officers do: "The ultimate goal of the police is to create a society that is free of crime and where everyone's rights are safe and secure." That broad mission entails a wide range of duties and responsibilities. Police officers' main duty is to enforce laws and protect people and property.

Uniformed police officers patrol assigned areas for suspicious activity or crimes being committed. They typically spend most of their workday patrolling on foot, riding a bicycle or motorcycle, or driving a car. The visible presence in the community of uniformed officers serves as a deterrent to anyone wanting to commit a crime. Police officers also go to crime scenes to aid victims, issue citations to people who violate traffic laws, and answer calls about possible

At a Glance:
Police Officer

Minimum Educational Requirements
High school diploma or equivalent; college experience or degree sometimes preferred

Personal Qualities
Self-confidence, problem-solving skills, physical bravery, integrity, works well with others

Certification and Licensing
Completion of police training academy

Working Conditions
Office setting; on patrol; various locations

Salary Range
Median annual salary of $60,270 in 2015

Number of Jobs
About 806,400 jobs in 2014

Future Job Outlook
Expected growth of 4 percent through 2024

crimes or emergencies people are having. Officers pursue or physically restrain crime suspects to make arrests, which can be dangerous. They also protect citizens by controlling large and sometimes violent crowds and responding to emergencies like severe weather such as floods.

All police officers do a lot of paperwork. After finishing patrols or investigating crimes, they return to headquarters and fill out reports on arrests, emergency response calls, and other activities they were involved in. They also write down things they saw or heard that can alert other officers to possible crimes or dangers to the community.

No day in the life of a police officer is exactly the same. One officer who described his experience as a police officer in Florida said a typical day might involve stopping a driver whose car has a missing headlight, responding to a serious car crash with injuries, informing next of kin a loved one has died in a crash, dealing with teenagers creating a disturbance at a gas station, responding to a possible burglary, and writing reports of his day's activities. "Working as a police officer brings on a range of emotions," Major Timothy Roufa writes in "A Day in the Life of a Police Officer" on the About.com website. "It can leave you feeling satisfied, rewarded, sad, disgruntled, lonely and fulfilled, all in the same shift."

How Do You Become a Police Officer?

Education

A high school degree or equivalent is the minimum education for a police officer. However, some police departments prefer applicants with college experience or even a four-year degree. Most colleges offer classes and degree programs in criminal justice for people who want to become police officers. Students learn about criminal law, how courts handle criminal cases, and police procedures. William Terrill teaches criminology at Michigan State University. In 2015 Terrill coauthored a study that found college education helps prepare new officers for police work, which can be daunting at first because rookie officers are often assigned to high-crime areas to gain experience. Terrill said college courses help officers develop analytical skills so they can better handle situations that confront them. An example is how much force to use to subdue subjects or whether to use force at all, depending on whether someone is committing a crime or only being a public nuisance by loitering.

Certification and Licensing

No matter what their education, new police officers are required to attend and pass an academy course that police forces operate to train recruits. Such courses usually last nineteen weeks. Training includes classroom instruction about state and local laws, constitutional law, civil rights, and police ethics. Trainees learn how to interact with people from different cultures, backgrounds, and sexual orientations to ensure good community relations. Recruits are taught to use various firearms, patrol areas, and search cars and buildings for evidence. They also learn how to subdue and arrest people, including when it is proper to employ deadly force. Physical training helps candidates increase their strength and fitness, and they also learn self-defense techniques.

Volunteer Work and Internships

Some police departments offer cadet programs that help young people decide if police work is a good career choice. Candidates usually have to be eighteen years old. Such programs vary from city to city but include training in police techniques. They also offer candidates opportunities to perform minor tasks like assisting officers with road hazards and riding along with officers on patrol to gain experience. Some programs are full time; others are part time. Some include pay; others do not. The New York Police Department Cadet Program, for instance, enables students to experience police work during the summer, when they are not attending school; they can also earn an hourly wage plus $10,000 in tuition assistance. Whether a cadet program is paid or unpaid, participation helps candidates get hired as police officers when they reach age twenty-one.

Skills and Personality

Police officers need many mental and physical attributes to be successful. Larry E. Capps was an assistant chief of the Missouri (Texas) Police Department. In a 2014 article for the *FBI Law Enforcement*

Bulletin, Capps wrote, "The internal desire to make the community better by protecting and serving should drive police applicants." Capps also said officers need initiative to act on their own even in dangerous situations, a sense of ethics about their actions, respect for and knowledge of the law, good communication skills, and the ability to control their tempers. And they must never forget that their job is to serve and protect citizens. Police officers also need physical strength, courage, and intelligence to make instantaneous life-or-death decisions. Another requirement is mental toughness, because officers experience many difficult situations in the course of their job. They see the bad sides of humanity most people never encounter. This includes responding to reports of domestic violence, sexual assault, or drug addicts or homeless people in life-or-death situations. Officers also witness people who are injured or dead from car crashes, beatings, and drive-by shootings. Their job may include being attacked by a drug-crazed or angry individual or a criminal trying to escape arrest.

Police officers are the most familiar face of law enforcement. They patrol neighborhoods, write traffic citations, respond to emergencies, and make arrests.

On the Job

Employers

Police officers work for local and state government agencies. The vast majority of officers work for police departments, with the number of officers depending on the city's population. New York City in 2016 had more than 35,000 uniformed officers, while Terre Haute, Indiana, had 136. Other police officers work for counties and are usually known as deputy sheriffs. They patrol county roads and sometimes provide police protection for smaller communities, especially in rural areas. States have police forces that patrol state and US highways and cooperate with other law enforcement agencies on criminal matters or to provide emergency services. No matter what level of government they work for or what they are called, law enforcement personnel perform the same basic function police officers do to protect citizens.

Working Conditions

When officers respond to 9-1-1 calls, they never know what they will find. In July 2015 Michael Castillo, a uniformed officer in Ansonia, Connecticut, was dispatched to break up a fight at a Target store. Instead of violence, Castillo found two boys trying to fix a broken bike. When Castillo helped the boys fix the bike, a woman took a picture of his kind act and posted it on Facebook. The post went viral, and Castillo was showered with praise. Officers sometimes save lives. Brian Strockbine is a police officer in Evesham, New Jersey. In just a ten-day period in 2016, he saved the lives of three people. On March 8 Strockbine responded to a report of a woman who was lying on a front lawn. When Strockbine got there, the woman was not breathing, but he administered cardiopulmonary resuscitation (CPR) to revive her. In a story on the NJ.com website, Strockbine said he was grateful he could help: "We don't do this job to be thanked or for the recognition. I love being a police officer and that day made me so proud." Only four days later Strockbine pulled a person from a burning car, and on March 17 he used CPR again to save another woman's life.

Being a police officer can be extremely stressful. Police officers

14

can never be sure what will happen when they respond to a call. And they know that dealings with suspects can become violent or deadly at any time. On February 27, 2016, Ashley Guindon was one of three officers responding to a call about a domestic disturbance in Prince William County, Virginia. When Guindon arrived at the home, she was shot to death by a man who had already killed his wife. It was Guindon's first day as a police officer.

Officers responding to reports of crimes often experience another very difficult part of police work—psychological and emotional anguish from watching victims of shootings or car accidents die. In a 2015 story on television station KMBC, Kansas City, Missouri, police officer Darren Ivy admitted, "It's not a natural thing to go to work every day and see people dying." Officers also may struggle emotionally when they encounter crime victims who are frightened and upset after being robbed, beaten, or raped. Many police departments, Kansas City's among them, teach officers psychological techniques to cope with such traumatic events.

Earnings

In May 2015 the Bureau of Labor Statistics reported the median annual salary for police officers was $60,270. The lowest 10 percent of such salaries averaged $34,170 and the highest 10 percent $100,560. Officers working in large cities usually earn more than those in smaller cities. In 2016 a police officer in Milwaukee, Wisconsin, with five years of experience earned $49,439, while a police officer in New York City with the same experience earned $60,209.

Opportunities for Advancement

Police officers begin their careers patrolling areas, but if they are skilled at their job, they have opportunities to assume more responsibility. Promotions to a higher rank and pay are based on test scores about law enforcement knowledge and reports on how officers have done their jobs. Police officers can seek promotion to detective, a job that requires more experience and skill and pays more. Detectives, who are known as plainclothes officers because they wear civilian clothing instead of uniforms, take the lead in investigating crimes.

They interview witnesses and suspects and use many types of evidence such as fingerprints, computers, and security videos to discover who committed crimes. When detectives identify suspects, they search for and arrest them. To learn about crimes or criminal groups, detectives sometimes work undercover. They assume a different identity as a means to gain information that cannot be obtained through more traditional channels. Officers can also advance to positions in specialized units like SWAT teams. Experienced officers can apply for jobs with higher-level state or federal law enforcement agencies like the Minnesota Bureau of Criminal Apprehension or the Drug Enforcement Administration.

What Is the Future Outlook for Police Officers?

Police officer jobs are expected to grow by 4 percent through 2024—lower than the predicted 6.5 percent growth rate for all jobs in that period. Members of minority groups and women may have a greater chance of being hired because police departments want to increase the diversity of their workforces.

Find Out More

Criminal Justice USA
website: www.criminaljusticeusa.com

This website has information on starting a law enforcement career, including educational and job opportunities in all fifty states.

Discover Policing
website: http://discoverpolicing.org

This website, managed by the International Association of Chiefs of Police, explores law enforcement careers, including education, what such jobs are like, and issues related to being a police officer.

Go Law Enforcement
website: www.golawenforcement.com

This website by retired law enforcement officer Joe Libowsky explains how to start a law enforcement career, including required education, the hiring process, and how to search for such jobs.

Officer.com
website: www.officer.com

This website has information on careers, education and training, technology, and issues concerning police work.

PoliceOne.com
website: www.policeone.com

Information on this website includes media articles on policing as well as articles and videos that discuss education, careers, and continued training.

Real Police
website: www.realpolice.net

This website offers articles and blogs, videos, job postings, and forums about police work.

Crime Scene Investigator

What Does a Crime Scene Investigator Do?

Crime scene investigators (CSIs) are also known as forensic scientists or crime scene technicians. Their job is to use science and technology to solve criminal cases. Henry C. Lee is one of the world's most famous crime scene investigators and founder of the prestigious Henry C. Lee Institute of Forensic Science at the University of New Haven in Connecticut. Lee says stories featuring fictional detective Sherlock Holmes helped introduce the use of scientific methods to collect and analyze evidence—methods that are still used today to solve real crimes. In a 2013 PBS television show titled *How Sherlock Changed the World*, Lee stated, "Sherlock Holmes is the grandfather of forensic science. Today when I go to a crime scene I use his logic, his method of deduction. That's how we do it today, solving cases based on Sherlock Holmes' logic." The popular stories by Sir Arthur Conan Doyle pioneered the most important rule in forensic science—that crime scenes be left undisturbed until investigators get there to preserve any physical evidence. This is how crime scenes are treated today. This is because moving the position of a body or weapon or contaminating the area with fingerprints or hair follicles, for example, can make it harder to understand what happened or pinpoint suspects.

The first things investigators do at crime scenes is take photographs or record a video of the site and any visible evidence so they have a visual record to refer to as they investigate the crime. They may also draw sketches and record initial observations such as where a body, weapon, or other evidence was found to document the crime scene's physical aspects. They collect weapons, fingerprints, bodily fluids, computers, and other evidence for further analysis. They write down their findings and conclusions in reports for detectives investigating the crime and for possible use in trials. Investigators in smaller law enforcement agencies will collect and analyze many different types of evidence. But investigators in larger departments may have specific areas of expertise, such as ballistics, fingerprinting, handwriting, or biochemistry.

One of the most important tasks investigators face is to carefully document where and how they obtain each piece of evidence. The legal phrase "chain of custody" refers to official records about how physical evidence was seized, how it was transferred to other law enforcement officials, how it was analyzed, and where and how it was eventually stored. Investigators must detail who handled every bit of evidence and what they did to ensure it was not tampered with. Judges may exclude evidence from being used in a trial if investigators fail to follow strict procedures in handling it.

Investigators take evidence back to their office and scientifically analyze it in a laboratory setting using microscopes, chemicals, as well as more high-tech methods. The goal is to learn as much as possible from the evidence about the crime and who may have committed it. Fingerprints are examined and compared to those in various databases in hopes of identifying the person who made them. A bullet has microscopic markings that can identify the gun from which it was fired. The markings can sometimes also determine if the gun was used in other crimes. DNA in hair fibers, blood, or other bodily fluids can help identify suspects. Even minute residue left behind when someone touches an object can contain enough DNA for possible identification in the lab. CSIs sometimes consult with outside experts more knowledgeable about evidence such as bite marks, edged weapons like swords, or poisons.

How Do You Become a Crime Scene Investigator?

Education

CSIs must have a bachelor's degree in any of a wide variety of subjects, including chemistry, biology, physics, or forensic science. A bachelor's degree in forensic science includes a wide range of course material and can help graduates get jobs in this field. In addition to learning how to use scientific methods to investigate crimes, the course work includes topics like morality in criminal justice and criminal justice administration. College courses in mathematics, statistics, and writing will ensure applicants have the skills necessary to write detailed reports that can be used as evidence in criminal trials. Advanced degrees in pathology, anthropology, or psychiatry are necessary for certain positions.

Certification and Licensing

There is a wide range of licenses and certificates available to prove applicants have the knowledge to work as investigators. The American Board of Criminalistics offers certificates to validate expertise applicants have as investigators. However, standards and requirements for investigators vary from one law enforcement agency to another.

Volunteer Work and Internships

The American Academy of Forensic Sciences holds several CSI Summer Camps for interested high school students. The camps offer hands-on experience in forensic science, including how to gather

A crime scene investigator gathers evidence in connection with a police shooting. CSIs scientifically evaluate evidence that may be used to solve crimes.

fingerprints and other evidence at crime scenes and how to conduct tests in the lab. The FBI, Naval Criminal Investigative Service, and US Secret Service offer internships (some paid, some unpaid) to college students majoring in criminology, criminal justice, or forensics. Students must be seniors or graduate students to qualify. Interns will gain experience in collecting evidence to discover facts about crimes.

Skills and Personality

CSIs rely on an array of skills and traits to do their job. A healthy curiosity about how things work or why something happens is important because that is the basis of their work. Critical-thinking and problem-solving skills are also essential. When they first view crime scenes, investigators must quickly decide what evidence to collect and the best way to do that. They also need to be proficient in taking careful, detailed notes and writing reports, which provide other law enforcement personnel with crucial information about what might have taken place and who might have been involved. These notes and reports are also used as evidence in trials. Physical fitness is another useful quality because CSIs sometimes spend long hours processing crime scenes. Finally, anyone who has an interest in this type of work must be able to endure the sight and smell of dead or mutilated bodies and other unpleasant aspects of bloody crime scenes.

On the Job

Employers

Law enforcement agencies at different levels of government hire CSIs. Police departments in big cities like New York and state and federal law enforcement agencies like the FBI will have entire departments devoted to CSI work. Within those large departments, individual investigators may specialize in analyzing specific types of evidence like bullets or fingerprints. Some smaller law enforcement agencies, especially those in rural areas, may not have any CSIs. They have to depend on other law enforcement agencies at the county or state level to help them when a crime requires CSI work.

Working Conditions

CSI: Crime Scene Investigation debuted on television in 2000. The show depicting how CSIs solve crimes was so popular that it ran for fifteen years and spawned several other similar series. Television, however, often bears little resemblance to reality, and real-world CSIs have complained that the shows make solving crimes look far too easy. Various law enforcement agencies conduct camps for youth in an effort to give them a more realistic picture of this work. In June 2016 several law enforcement agencies, including the FBI, conducted a five-day CSI Forensic Science Camp in Anchorage, Alaska, for high school students. In a television interview, former Alaska state trooper Steven Arlow said campers learned that CSI work is much harder and more time-consuming than it appears on television: "A lot of our kids see things on TV like 'CSI' and in 30 minutes and two commercials, they've solved the homicide and that's not reality."

The reality of CSI work is that it takes a lot of time to collect, analyze, and assess evidence. This can be seen in real-world crime scenes all the time. In April 2016 when investigators arrived at the scene of a murder in Oxon Hill, Maryland, the first thing they did was put on latex gloves and lightweight suits covering their bodies. The suits prevented them from contaminating evidence with their DNA or anything else they might carry into the scene. Investigators started by making sketches and a visual record of the crime scene, including the victim, a man shot to death in the bedroom of an apartment. Their search for a bullet included sawing into a wall because of an apparent bullet hole, but none was found. Investigators bagged a variety of items, including a shell casing, cigarette butts, drug paraphernalia, and beer cans, to test them for DNA and fingerprints. So it takes many hours of painstaking searching to gather evidence. In a *Washington Post* story on their work, First Sergeant Charles Montgomery commented that even though the apartment was small, "it's going to be one of those extra long nights."

One of the hardest parts of crime scene investigation is the emotional trauma investigators experience in working gruesome crime scenes. Dena Weiss is a CSI and fingerprint expert for the Lakeland, Florida, police department. In a story on the PoliceOne.com website, Weiss explained how difficult it had been for her to process a crime scene in which a mother killed her young daughter and then committed suicide: "The violent death of a child is horrific to deal with. We spent more than nine hours at that crime scene. It haunted me for a long time." The unpleasantness of crime scenes assaults the senses in many different ways. Jim Dees is a former investigator for the Reno, Nevada, police department. In a post on Quora, Dees said the smell of decomposing bodies is always awful, but "the most difficult part of the job for me was the bugs." Flies and other insects feed on dead bodies and lay eggs, resulting in maggots that investigators sometimes must brush away to find evidence.

Once evidence is recovered, investigators move their work to laboratory settings, where they use scientific methods to painstakingly examine and document evidence to solve crimes and prosecute suspects. The scientific procedures investigators employ will enable them to learn specific and important facts about crimes. For example, did blood or DNA on a knife come from the stabbing victim or a possible suspect?

Earnings

The median annual pay for CSIs in 2015 was $56,310. The lowest-paid 10 percent earned less than $34,000 and the highest 10 percent more than $94,410. CSIs often have opportunities for overtime to increase their earnings.

Opportunities for Advancement

CSIs can be promoted to positions of higher authority, like heading a team or an entire department. They can study and become experts in specialized fields like ballistics; they can also move to larger, more prestigious law enforcement agencies. Some investigators with reputations for expertise in analyzing crime scenes may decide to quit their jobs and become expert witnesses who are paid to testify in trials about evidence. Attorneys for either the prosecution or defense often hire CSIs to testify as expert witnesses in trials. Such work can often pay better than working as an investigator.

What Is the Future Outlook for Crime Scene Investigators?

Crime scene investigator is a rapidly growing occupation, and the number of jobs is expected to grow by 27 percent through 2024—far higher than the predicted 6.5 percent growth rate for all jobs in that period. That is due to rising crime rates and the increasing effectiveness of solving crimes through the scientific analysis of crime scene data.

Find Out More

CrimeSceneInvestigatorEDU.org
website: crimesceneinvestigatoredu.org

This site has information on CSI careers, education, certification, and salaries. It also offers information on a large sampling of careers in forensic science.

Forensics Colleges
website: www.forensicscolleges.com

This site has information on colleges and degree programs (including online programs) for those interested in a career as a crime scene investigator or working in other areas of forensic science.

International Crime Scene Investigators Association (ICSIA)
website: www.icsia.org

This is an industry organization that supports those who work in crime scene investigation. The website has information on certification and training, tools used by CSIs in their work, and a link to an article titled "How to Become a CSI."

National Forensic Science Technology Center (NFSTC)
website: www.nfstc.org

The NFSTC provides training, assessment, research, and technology assistance to the justice and forensic communities. Its website offers free guides to crime scene investigation, a simplified discussion of forensic science, and information about career opportunities.

Emergency Dispatcher

At a Glance:

Emergency Dispatcher

Minimum Educational Requirements
High school diploma or equivalent

Personal Qualities
Good listener, able to multitask and make quick life-or-death decisions, able to handle the emotional stress of emergency situations

Working Conditions
Office setting; on the telephone

Salary Range
Median annual salary of $38,101 in 2015

Number of Jobs
About 102,000 jobs in 2015

Future Job Outlook
A 3 percent decline in jobs predicted through 2024

An elderly man feels pain shooting up his arm and thinks he is having a heart attack. A woman hears glass breaking and believes an intruder is invading her home. Thick, acrid smoke awakens a mom and dad, who collect their children and flee their burning house. In all three scenarios, the people immediately call 9-1-1 to plead for help to save them from a life-threatening situation. The person they will speak to is an emergency dispatcher, or public safety telecommunicator. All 9-1-1 calls go to emergency dispatch centers known in the United States and Canada as Public-Safety Answering Points (PSAPs). The centers are operated at the city or county level so dispatchers will be able to quickly dispatch help wherever and whenever it is needed. In 2016 there were more than six thousand PSAPs in the United States. Dispatchers working in those centers handle an estimated 240 million calls annually. The goal of emergency dispatchers is to get help to callers or the people for whom they are calling as quickly as possible—all in an effort to save lives.

The first thing a dispatcher has to do is decide if the call is legitimate. Pranksters, many of them teenagers, sometimes call with made-up stories (a crime that can lead to arrest and charges). High school students, for example, have phoned in bomb threats to schools in hopes of getting a day off. People also sometimes mistakenly dial 9-1-1 centers while trying to call about legitimate nonemergency situations. After dispatchers assess the validity of the call, they begin asking the caller a series of questions to find out exactly what happened, a task that is often difficult because the people calling may be so afraid or emotionally upset that they have trouble giving coherent answers. The first piece of information dispatchers need is the location of callers so they can send help to the right place. This task is vitally important but not always easy. Dispatchers will immediately know the address of callers using landline telephones because those numbers automatically pop up on a computer screen in front of them. In some cities and counties, dispatchers have computer programs that pinpoint exactly where cell phone calls are coming from, but many do not. The closest dispatchers can get without those programs is the cell tower nearest the caller. Dispatchers in those areas must spend precious time getting accurate information about a caller's location. Dispatchers ask other questions about the exact nature of the emergency so they can decide which first-responder agency to contact. They must also assess the severity of the emergency from the caller's statements so they can have the appropriate agency respond accordingly. For example, a fire in an apartment complex requires more firefighters and equipment than one in a single-family home.

After notifying the proper agency, dispatchers may stay on the line with callers to calm them down. They may advise callers on how to stay safe or how to handle the emergency themselves until help arrives. An example of this is when dispatchers receive calls from depressed or angry people who say they want to commit suicide or kill someone. Dispatchers try to talk callers out of doing that or at least keep them on the phone talking until first responders arrive to handle the situation in person. Dispatchers also monitor responses to calls they receive to make sure callers are being helped. Dispatchers in the Milwaukee Police Department, for example, can view an electronic map that shows responses to 9-1-1 calls; information on responses is updated every fifteen minutes to show what is happening in each situation. When necessary, dispatchers work with other dispatchers or law enforcement personnel to coordinate responses to emergency calls. Dispatchers must also keep detailed records of every call they receive.

Modern technology makes this job easier, but it is not always easy for dispatchers to deal with that technology. Cindra Dunaway is a dispatcher for the Fort Myers, Florida, police department. In a post on the Association of Public Safety Communications Officials website, Dunaway wrote, "We have multiple screens in front of us every day and are required to know how to operate and monitor all of them." Thus, mastering and using several types of computers or other technological devices at the same time is challenging.

How Do You Become an Emergency Dispatcher?

Education and Training

The minimum education required for entry-level police, fire, and ambulance emergency dispatchers is a high school diploma or equivalent. Postsecondary education in law enforcement or emergency dispatching is generally not necessary for applicants. However, college courses or degrees in several majors, including public safety or emergency management, can increase the chance of being hired. Past experience in law enforcement, firefighting, or medical care can also help applicants win jobs.

Emergency dispatchers will be trained to do their jobs by their employer or a national association involved in that field that trains dispatchers for local governments. Applicants who successfully complete training sometimes receive certificates proving their competence. Various local, state, and federal levels of government require different levels of training.

Skills and Personality

The most important trait emergency dispatchers need is being able to remain calm while handling calls from people involved in traumatic situations. They have to be able to think quickly to decide the best way to respond to a panicked caller. Empathy, or the ability to understand another person's experiences and emotions, is another essential trait for an emergency dispatcher. An empathetic dispatcher has a better chance of calming callers who are frightened, angry, or distraught and getting the information first responders will need once they arrive on the scene. Strong communication skills, both verbal and written, are essential, as is the ability to do several things at once. Dispatchers are multitaskers—they get information from callers about their emergency while also contacting first responders while also reassuring callers while also taking notes of events as they unfold.

On the Job

Employers

Most emergency dispatchers—81 percent in 2014, according to the Bureau of Labor Statistics—work for local law enforcement agencies and fire departments. Some dispatchers work for state governments or for private companies.

Working Conditions

Because 9-1-1 calls can come in at any time, dispatchers may have to work evenings, weekends, and holidays. They may also have to work rotating shifts that can disrupt sleep patterns and their private lives. Some agencies work dispatchers in shifts of ten or twelve hours instead of the standard eight hours to make it easier to schedule round-the-clock coverage.

Being a dispatcher involves much more than just answering calls. Kimberly Matos works for the Linden, New Jersey, police department. In an April 4, 2016, post on the National Public Safety Telecommunicators Week website that honors dispatchers, she wrote, "We are not just call takers, we are 'Life Savers.' I still can't believe I

An emergency dispatcher responds to calls. Dispatchers must calm panicked callers to determine the nature of the emergency and which first responders to send. They also gather information that will be crucial for a speedy and efficient response.

have saved lives numerous times, that I talked someone out of wanting to commit suicide."

Unlike police officers or other members of the law enforcement community, dispatchers do not go to crime or accident scenes. As part of their interactions with callers, however, they regularly experience emotional trauma. In 2014 Carl Simpson was a director of Denver's 9-1-1 call center. In a 2014 post on the *Badge of Life Canada* blog, Simpson wrote, "As call takers we hear beatings, shootings, gasping, screaming, swearing, crying, rounds being fired, silence and then tears and sobbing. [We] hear people take their last breath." In a 2014 interview with ABC News, Georgia 9-1-1 supervisor Elaina Fincher discussed the difficult emotions dispatchers can experience. Fincher said callers have told her, "Hey, I just stabbed my husband in the chest and he's bleeding." She adds, "Having a person call and say their 5-year-old child's leg was just amputated by a bear trap . . . stuff like that just sticks with you." Fincher said dealing with such callers can be emotionally upsetting on many different levels.

Sometimes the calls become deeply personal. Matos once received a call that a young woman had been shot. The shooting happened near her home, and she feared her daughter might have been the victim. Although her daughter was not involved, Matos later learned the victim was one of her daughter's friends. And when major disasters like floods or fires endanger homes where dispatchers live, they cannot leave their jobs to check on their own home because they are needed more than ever to answer calls.

A Northern Illinois University study concluded that emergency dispatchers are at risk of developing post-traumatic stress disorder because of the emotional strain they experience on the job. A university news release about the study's finding began, "For most people, it's the stuff of nightmares. For busy 9-1-1 emergency dispatchers, it's all in a day's work." The study authors noted that dispatchers have no time to stop and process emotionally heartrending situations they experience secondhand because they are busy responding to them. The authors added that a powerful mix of emotions resulting from those calls can lead to depression in some who do this work. To help dispatchers deal with stress, some agencies have switched to shorter work shifts.

Even though emergency dispatchers save lives and experience traumatic incidents secondhand, they do their work in relative anonymity. As a result, many dispatchers feel they are not appreciated as much as other members of law enforcement. In a 2013 *Washington Post* newspaper story, Arlington, Virginia, dispatcher Vanessa Coles said, "When the mayor and the sheriff and the chief of police stand up [and thank officers and firefighters] I would just love to hear someone say, 'I would like to thank all the dispatchers, all the call-takers.'"

Earnings

In May 2015 the median annual wage for emergency dispatchers was $38,101. The bottom 10 percent earned $24,270 and the top 10 percent $59,770. However overtime can boost dispatcher salaries, and there are usually many opportunities to work overtime.

Opportunities for Advancement

Emergency dispatchers who excel at their work can win promotion to higher-level positions, including managing other dispatchers. One way that dispatchers can do that is to take classes and training courses in their field beyond the minimum required for their job. The extra knowledge and skills they acquire will improve the work they do and lead to more responsible positions.

What Is the Future Outlook for Emergency Dispatchers?

The number of emergency dispatcher jobs is declining. The Bureau of Labor Statistics predicts a 3 percent decline in jobs through 2024, which means three thousand fewer emergency dispatchers. The decrease is due to new technologies that will allow fewer people to handle more calls. However, turnover in this profession is high, which means jobs will be available despite a decline in numbers. In 2013 the *Journal of Emergency Dispatch* reported that 17 percent to 19 percent of dispatchers leave the profession annually. This presents an opportunity for anyone who is interested in getting into this line of work.

Find Out More

International Academies of Emergency Dispatch
website: www.emergencydispatch.org

The academy was started in 1988 to set standards for handling emergency medical dispatch calls and now includes fire and police emergencies. It has a range of articles and data on ethics, certification, and other aspects of dispatch work.

Journal of Emergency Dispatch
website: www.iaedjournal.org

This is an online resource for news, features, and comments about emergency dispatching.

National Emergency Number Association (NENA)
website: www.nena.org

NENA has nine thousand members in the United States and worldwide. Its website has information on education, training, and statistics related to emergency dispatch.

National Public Safety Telecommunicators Week
website: www.npstw.org

The second week of April each year is set aside to honor emergency dispatchers. This website includes newspaper stories and posts about dispatchers and this career.

911 DispatcherEDU.org
website: www.911dispatcheredu.org

This site has information on required education for dispatchers, certification, and links to schools that teach dispatch protocols.

FBI Special Agent

At a Glance:
FBI Special Agent

Minimum Educational Requirements

A four-year college degree plus three years of professional work experience

Personal Qualities

Physical bravery, good communication skills, sound judgment, ability to work as a team with others

Certification and Licensing

Pass the FBI Basic Field Training Courses and other classes at the FBI Academy in Quantico, Virginia

Working Conditions

Office and field settings

Salary Range

Median annual salary of $63,595 in 2016

Number of Jobs

More than 13,500 special agent positions in 2015

Future Job Outlook

Expected growth of 4 percent through 2024, lower than average for all occupations

What Does an FBI Special Agent Do?

As the primary law enforcement agency for the US government, the FBI enforces more than two hundred categories of federal law and is considered the nation's premier law enforcement agency. Since its creation in 1908, the FBI has battled crime domestically and in foreign nations where criminal activity affects the United States. FBI special agents seek and apprehend a wide range of criminals, including sexual predators, serial murderers, corrupt government officials, cyber- and technology criminals, and those who profit from economic crimes. Agents also protect the civil rights of US citizens. Although the FBI is the investigative arm of the US Department of Justice, it works with law enforcement agencies throughout the nation to solve crimes and arrest individuals suspected of committing crimes.

Since the September 11, 2001, terrorist attacks, agents have also been fighting terrorism. In an April 4, 2016, report on TV station WIVD in Buffalo, New York, FBI director James Comey emphasized the importance of combating domestic and foreign acts of terrorism. Comey said his agents are constantly "trying to spot and assess people and if they're on a path towards violence to disrupt them." The FBI also cooperates with the CIA and other US and foreign intelligence agencies to locate and stop terrorists, spies, or others from threatening national security.

John Jeffries is a former FBI special agent in Portland, Oregon. Jeffries says that working as an FBI special agent is not as exciting as TV shows and movies portray it. Instead of engaging in car chases and shoot-outs, a typical agent spends most of his or her time on painstaking searches for evidence of crimes and other threats to the nation. Such searches often turn up small bits of evidence that, when gathered together, can document how crimes are being committed. "It is the detail that allows the FBI to put together large cases that end with placing handcuffs on the subject," Jeffries wrote in a post on the Portland FBI website. Agents hunt for those important details in many ways. They execute search warrants of homes and businesses, meet with informants with knowledge of criminal or terrorist activity, and interview suspects or other people for additional useful details.

On any particular day, agents may handle a wide variety of other tasks, including making arrests and testifying in trials. Some agents do background checks on people applying for positions in federal agencies, while others specialize in training other agents, forensics, or public affairs. Their daily routine also includes paperwork since they must file reports on their activities and progress in investigations.

How Do You Become an FBI Special Agent?

Education

Applicants need a four-year college degree. Some applicants study law enforcement or criminology, but a wide variety of degrees, including finance and accounting, are acceptable. Applicants must also have worked three years in their major or field of study to show they can put what they learned to practical use.

Certification and Licensing

Competition for acceptance as a special agent candidate is strong. The FBI's website says that in 2014 it received over twenty thousand applications for approximately seven hundred special agent vacancies. Candidates must attend the FBI Academy in Quantico, Virginia, and pass the Basic Field Training Course. The course, which is approximately eight hundred hours, teaches applicants how to conduct investigations, interview people, and provide briefings to others on what they learned or accomplished on duty. The course teaches individual agents how to work efficiently with fellow agents and other law enforcement officers. Academic training ends with criminal and counterterrorism exercises based on real-life situations such as negotiating with people holding hostages and arresting armed suspects. Training includes instruction in firearms, driving skills for vehicular pursuits, and tactical situations like how to safely and efficiently search buildings for evidence or armed suspects.

Volunteer Work and Internships

The FBI Honors Internship Program allows college students to experience what it is like to work for the FBI. It is open to students who have completed at least two semesters of college and are attending college full-time. During the ten-week program from June to August, interns work forty hours a week with FBI employees. Interns are paid a salary tied to their education level and must pay personal travel, housing, and other expenses associated with the internship. Interns who perform well may have the opportunity to work sixteen hours a month for the FBI during the school year. The experience interns get will not guarantee them a job with the FBI when they graduate, but it might help—especially in terms of making personal contacts and having a clearer understanding of the work.

Skills and Personality

Among the most important qualities for an FBI special agent are good interpersonal and communication skills, sound judgment, integrity, a respect for laws, and the ability to work with a team or partner. FBI agents must also be physically fit and experienced in using firearms. Agents must have good decision-making skills and be able to make instantaneous choices in dangerous situations, including those involving life and death.

On the Job

Employers

All special agents work directly for the FBI, a US government agency.

Working Conditions

The FBI has fifty-six field offices throughout the United States and one in San Juan, Puerto Rico. Agents can wind up living and working in tropical Honolulu, Hawaii, or frigid Anchorage, Alaska, where the temperature can dip to -50°F (-46°C) and FBI equipment includes snowmobiles. The majority of special agents work in larger cities like New York City, Los Angeles, Chicago, Houston, and Atlanta. As with any law enforcement position, agents may work different shifts during a twenty-four-hour period. And during emergencies or other peak periods, agents may have to work long hours and even forgo days off.

There is no typical day for agents, because they have a wide variety of duties, some of which are dangerous. Some agents spend most of their working day in offices collecting and analyzing information from various sources to piece together criminal or terrorist plots. Other agents spend more time in the field interviewing people, including informants, and seeking information on cases they are investigating. Agents work with other agents while investigating cases assigned to them. For example, they work closely with FBI intelligence analysts, who gather information from many sources, including human intelligence (known as HUMINT) from interviews with people, other intelligence agencies, electronic and Internet surveillance, interrogations, and non-FBI criminal investigations.

Agents' lives may be endangered when they arrest people or raid locations involving illegal or terrorist activity. Undercover assignments in which agents pretend to be criminals or terrorists are the most dangerous work they do, because their lives are at risk if people they are investigating learn their true identity. Agents need special skills for such work. From 1988 to 2012, FBI agent Kingman Wong's Asian heritage and ability to speak Chinese enabled him to investigate criminal gangs in the United States, Hong Kong, and Thailand. In a 2015 story on the FBI website, Kingman said, "In terms of infiltrating these groups, you have to know the culture, you have to know the language."

Fighting terrorism is another top priority for agents. For example, the FBI worked with a Joint Terrorist Task Force in Rochester, New York, to successfully prosecute Mufid Elfgeeh of New York. He was sentenced in March 2016 to more than twenty-two years in prison for recruiting supporters for the Muslim extremist group Islamic State of Iraq and the Levant, or ISIL. In a May 16, 2016, FBI news release, an unidentified special agent said Elfgeeh was also planning to kill US military veterans: "He had stated, 'we kill them as they kill us.'"

The rapid growth of the Internet has forced the FBI to patrol a new area: cyberspace. Colleen Moss heads the FBI's Computer Analysis Response Team in Charlotte, North Carolina. In a 2015 report on TV station WBTV, Moss said her work encompasses a wide variety of Internet crime: "From gangs and drugs, all the way up to counter intelligence, counter terrorism, white collar fraud. All of those types of cases have some type of digital media that needs to be reviewed." In one case, Moss posed as a child in Internet chat rooms to snare child pornographers and pedophiles. Agents monitor Internet communications for any illegal or terrorist activity and, with judicial approval, can tap telephones for the same purpose.

Special agents enjoy their work for many reasons. One is that they feel they are helping their nation by reducing crime and keeping it safe from terrorists and others. There is also the satisfaction of working for a law enforcement agency that is respected and has a long, rich history. Agents are also paid well and have good job benefits.

But there are also negatives to this job. Working as a special agent can be difficult emotionally because agents sometimes encounter dead bodies, victims of rape and beatings, or anguished parents whose children have been kidnapped. This job can also be dangerous. On May 24, 2016, two agents with an FBI SWAT team were wounded in a gunfight in Park Forest, Illinois, while arresting a high-ranking gang member.

The long and unusual hours agents work can negatively affect family life. Gary Noesner retired from the FBI in 2003 after three decades as an agent. In a 2015 *Business Insider* newspaper story, Noesner said the worst part of his job was "I was gone a lot—I traveled 25 percent to 30 percent of the time [as a hostage negotiator]—so my family kind of went on without me. I was a good father, I think. I tried to coach my kids' sports team and all that, but the reality was, I missed a lot of stuff."

But the difficult parts of the job have a positive side—shared hardships build strong personal bonds between agents that make it easier to endure such hardships. In a post on the Portland FBI website, former agent John Jeffries wrote, "The culture of the FBI is we are a family. A family takes care of each other and is there when help is needed." Jeffries said agents watch out for each other's safety in dangerous situations. And when fellow agents are having personal problems like illness, other agents donate sick or vacation days to help them.

Earnings

The salaries of agents are tied to the General Schedule for federal workers. Government employees climb the pay scale through seniority, experience, and promotions to higher-level jobs. New agents begin at the GS-10 level, which in 2016 was $47,158 annually. Median pay in 2016 was $63,595 and ranged up to $120,000 for the highest 10 percent. Agents also receive health care, pensions, and vacations.

Opportunities for Advancement

Agents can be promoted to jobs with greater responsibility as they gain experience or succeed in difficult investigations. The FBI offers agents the opportunity to learn new skills through in-house classes and outside educational opportunities that help them perform better and move up in rank.

What Is the Future Outlook for FBI Special Agents?

The number of FBI jobs is expected to grow by 4 percent through 2024, which is lower than the 6.5 percent average for all occupations. However, the FBI wants to hire more black and Latino agents in the future to create a more diverse agent population. In 2016 only 4.37 percent of FBI agents were black and 6.63 percent Latino. The FBI also wants to hire more female agents.

Find Out More

FBIAgentEDU.org
website: www.fbiagentedu.org

This website provides information about education, internships, job requirements, job duties, and salaries for FBI careers including agent jobs in areas ranging from counterintelligence to cybercrime.

FBI Agents Association (FBIAA)
website: www.fbiaa.org

This organization represents more than thirteen thousand active and retired FBI agents in areas involving career advancement, advocacy on budget issues, and more. Its website includes news stories on topics of interest to its members and anyone considering a career as an FBI agent.

Federal Bureau of Investigation (FBI)
website: www.fbi.gov

The agency's official website provides links to information about FBI careers and how students can prepare for them. It also describes the agency's Teen Academy and Youth Academy programs for high school students and provides details about the types of cases the agency investigates.

Correctional Officer

Correctional officers maintain order and supervise inmates in jails and prisons. Inmates who have not yet been charged with crimes, are awaiting trial, or have not yet been sentenced are usually held in city or county jails. People convicted of minor crimes and sentenced to short terms of incarceration may also serve their sentences in jails. Those convicted of more serious crimes and sentenced to several years in prison are housed in state or federal prisons. In either type of facility, correctional officers enforce rules, supervise inmates' daily activities, prevent fights and other physical assaults, keep inmates and anyone else in the correctional facility safe, and ensure that prisoners cannot escape. Officers occasionally have to search prisoners and inspect their cells and other areas of correctional facilities for contraband—items prisoners are not allowed to have, like cell phones, drugs, or anything that could be used as a weapon. Officers routinely inspect prison areas for signs of security breaches

At a Glance:
Correctional Officer

Minimum Educational Requirements

High school diploma or equivalent at state and local level; college degree and three years work experience at federal level

Personal Qualities

Good physical condition, ability to interact with people, strong communication skills, self-disciplined, patient, assertive

Working Conditions

Jails and prisons

Salary Range

Median annual salary of $40,530 in 2015

Number of Jobs

About 427,790 correctional officer and jailer jobs in 2015

Future Job Outlook

Projected 4 percent job growth through 2024

that could lead to escapes, like windows or bars prisoners have tampered with. Violations of prison or jail rules can lead to penalties for inmates—and heightened tension between correctional officers who report violations and inmates who are penalized. Correctional officers also monitor visits by lawyers, medical personnel, and family members of inmates; write reports about inmate behavior; and handle many types of paperwork, such as records of inmate medical needs.

Because correctional officers work in close proximity to prisoners, they are required to follow strict procedures aimed at keeping both guards and prisoners safe. Officers sometimes accompany prisoners from their cells to areas in the correctional facility set aside for medical care or authorized visits, or on trips outside the prison for court appearances and other valid reasons. On such trips, officers sometimes restrain inmates with handcuffs or leg shackles. If prisoners escape or commit a crime within the jail or prison, officers help officials investigate those crimes and search for escaped prisoners. However, correctional officers have no law enforcement powers outside their workplace.

How Do You Become a Correctional Officer?

Education and Training

A high school diploma or equivalent is the minimum required. Some state and local corrections agencies require college credits, but law enforcement or military experience may be substituted for that requirement. The Federal Bureau of Prisons requires entry-level corrections officers to have at least a bachelor's degree and three years' experience in a field providing counseling or supervision of individuals, such as teaching, alcohol and drug rehabilitation, or social work.

People accepted as correctional officers go through specialized training at schools run by law enforcement agencies and must pass required tests before they can start working in jails and prisons. Physical training teaches candidates how to use firearms and defend themselves in physical confrontations with prisoners. Learning how to keep prisons safe for both inmates and correctional officers is one of the most important parts of this training. For example, officers are taught to look for signs of depression or other psychological problems in inmate behavior in hopes of preventing violence and other problems. Candidates must also master the rules and regulations on policies and procedures of facilities they will work in. Correctional officers must be in good physical condition, and they may have to pass a test of their physical ability.

Volunteer Work and Internships

Internships are available for college students in some correctional facilities. For example, in 2016 the New York City Department of Corrections offered a five-week, paid summer intern program for students enrolled in a college or professional degree program such as criminal justice. Interns could be assigned to more than a dozen correctional programs in the New York department, including Youthful Offender Programming, Public Information, Investigations, and Training.

Skills and Personality

Individuals who want to work as correctional officers must possess certain skills and characteristics. Physical fitness is one. Other important attributes for this position include good judgment, self-discipline, resourcefulness, the ability to get along with different types of people, good verbal and written communication skills, tolerance, patience, and firmness. Deborah Ammeson worked for more than a decade at the Walworth County Jail in Wisconsin. In an interview posted on the All Criminal Justice Schools website, Ammeson said decisiveness and confidence are other essential qualities for correctional officers: "You have to react to a situation, and you have to believe that you know what you're doing and you have to do it. You have to be confident in your physical and mental ability to do it."

On the Job

Employers

Most correctional officers work in jails or prisons operated by local, state, or federal government agencies. State governments are the largest employer, with about 236,890 correctional officers employed in state penitentiaries. Local governments employ about 157,900 officers, and the federal government about 16,250. Some government agencies have contracted private businesses to operate their correctional facilities. A University of Wisconsin study showed that in 2015 the United States housed 10 percent of inmates in private prisons—20 percent of all federal prisoners and about 7 percent of state prisoners. However, in August 2016 the US Department of Justice said it would quit using private prisons in the future because they were less safe and effective in rehabilitating prisoners than those the government operated.

Working Conditions

Jails and prisons can be bleak places to work because they are built for one purpose—to incarcerate people. Their outer designs include tall, thick walls, iron bars, barbed wire, and electrified fences. The interiors feature an endless series of locked metal doors to prohibit inmate movement. Many older facilities are often unbearably hot in summer and cold in winter. And the job of a correctional officer can be very stressful and dangerous, especially when something happens to stir inmate emotions and things spiral out of control. This happened on March 11, 2016, at the William C. Holman Correctional Facility in Escambia County, Alabama, when inmates stabbed a corrections officer and warden during a prison riot. Nearly one hundred inmates started a fire and seized control of a dormitory area at the prison. The officer was stabbed while trying to break up a fight between two prisoners; the warden was stabbed when he arrived with other guards to assess the situation. Their wounds were not serious. But in an Associated Press story, State Senator Cam Ward commented, "Anybody who has been inside the facilities knows what a dangerous situation those officers work in every day."

In addition to danger from violent inmates, correctional officers risk exposure to contagious diseases. Some prisoners have AIDS, and officers have a slight risk of contracting the disease if they have to help an inmate who is bleeding. Some inmates with AIDS taunt officers by spitting on them to scare them; such outbursts are always punished. The twin dangers of violence and illness combine to give correctional officers one of the highest rates of injury and illness of any occupation.

A 2015 Bureau of Labor Statistics report said the overall rate of non-fatal occupational injury and illness cases requiring days away from work in 2014 was 107.1 per 10,000 full-time workers. But the rate for correctional officers was the highest of any state government job, with nearly 492 cases per 10,000 workers; only police officers experience a greater share of violent on-the-job encounters.

Correctional officers work in dangerous conditions for long periods. Most officers work eight-hour first, second, or third shifts, but some facilities require twelve-hour shifts. In addition, correctional officers often work overtime due to illness, vacations, or increased problems with inmates. Many officers welcome the chance to earn more money, but they are sometimes forced to work overtime because of staff shortages. Latisha Clements is a guard at a Michigan women's prison. In a 2016 *Oakland (Michigan) Press* newspaper story, Clements complained she had to work so much that it hurt her mental and physical health and her "ability to adequately care for my husband and children."

There is a lot of emotional stress due to working every day in a bleak setting guarding people convicted of terrible crimes like murder and sexual assault. Aaron Blair trains recruits for the Wyoming Department of Corrections. In a 2015 interview on National Public Radio, the former corrections officer admitted how difficult that is: "We know, going in those gates every day, we're dealing with convicted felons. It can wear on a person, become very dark."

Despite being difficult and dangerous, there are positive reasons to become a corrections officer. Mater Mea is a website featuring stories on black women who combine motherhood with various careers. In a 2014 post, Guimmara' Jones explained why she liked being a California prison guard: "I felt I could make an impact on society." Jones said some of her family members and friends had been incarcerated. Jones added that she knew many prisoners had just made mistakes in their lives, and she wanted a chance to help people rehabilitate themselves. Working in corrections is also a good job choice for people who want to be challenged every day when they go to work, because the personalities and situations in prisons are constantly changing and evolving. Some of them will be negative, but corrections officers are rarely bored.

Job security is something any worker values. In an interview on the All Criminal Justice Schools website, Deborah Ammeson said knowing that her job would not disappear was comforting: "It's been a good job, very stable. They're never going to run out of work."

Earnings

The median annual salary for a correctional officer in 2015 was $40,530, with the lowest 10 percent earning $27,830 and the top 10 percent more than $73,060. Pay and benefits in government and private prisons are comparable. Correction workers usually have the opportunity to work overtime to earn more money.

Opportunities for Advancement

Correctional officers begin in entry-level positions. As officers gain experience, they can advance to higher-level positions within their department as administrators in charge of other guards or specific programs. Correctional officers can even become wardens. Stanley Williams started as a corrections officer in Georgia but in 2016 became warden of Valdosta State Prison. Officers can also move to other jails or prisons for better pay or working conditions. The training and experience correctional officers have may allow them to move to other law enforcement positions like police officer.

What Is the Future Outlook for Correctional Officers?

Job growth through 2024 is expected to be 4 percent, which is lower than the predicted 6.5 percent growth rate for all jobs in that period. However the high turnover rate at some state and local prisons due to guards retiring, taking another job, or quitting means that there are often openings for this type of job.

Find Out More

Correctional OfficerEDU.org
website: www.correctionalofficeredu.org

This website features information on careers, training, and education for correctional officers.

Correctional Peace Officers Foundation
website: http://cpof.org

The foundation works to help correctional officers and their families; the website has information on this career.

Corrections One
website: www.correctionsone.com

This website provides corrections officers with information and resources that can help them in their profession, including print and video articles about corrections work.

Discover Corrections
website: http://discovercorrections.com

This website has information on careers in the field of corrections, including a section on why people want such jobs.

Border Patrol Agent

At a Glance:

Border Patrol Agent

Minimum Educational Requirements

A college degree; a combination of postsecondary education and military experience may also qualify

Personal Qualities

Good physical condition, able to deal with stressful situations, empathetic, good with people, speak Spanish or have the ability to learn a foreign language

Certification and Licensing

Must pass nineteen-week training course at Border Patrol Academy in New Mexico

Working Conditions

Mostly outdoors—patrolling in vehicles, on horseback, and on foot

Salary Range

Median annual salary of $64,000 in 2016

Number of Jobs

More than 20,000 positions in 2016

Future Job Outlook

Expected job growth of 4 percent through 2022, slower than the average for all jobs

What Does a Border Patrol Agent Do?

The US land border with Canada is 5,525 miles (8,891.6 km); the border with Mexico is 1,989 miles (3,200 km); and the US maritime border is 95,000 miles (152,887 km) of shoreline. Since 1924 the US Border Patrol has patrolled those borders to stop people from illegally entering the United States. Agents also fight crime and protect US citizens by stopping shipments of illegal weapons and drugs from entering the country. Since the terrorist attacks of September 11, 2001, the Border Patrol has also been involved in the fight to prevent terrorists and terrorist weapons from entering the United States.

Border Patrol agents guard the border in many ways—two of the main tactics are linewatch and signcutting. Linewatch refers to surveillance by agents of US land and sea borders to spot suspicious activity involving illegal smuggling of goods or illegal entry. One type of linewatch is to inspect vehicles crossing the border. On June 2, 2016, agents at a border checkpoint near Yuma, Arizona, seized nearly 13 pounds (6 kg) of cocaine from a vehicle after a drug-sniffing canine alerted them to the illegal drugs. Agents also use several types of electronic surveillance to linewatch, including sensor alarms at key border points and the Tethered Aerostat Radar System. The latter is a low-flying satellite system using radar emitted from blimps floating 10,000 feet (3,048 m) in the sky to spot illegal aircraft. The system stretches from Yuma, Arizona, to Lajas, Puerto Rico. Linewatch also uses drones to patrol US borders. Signcutting involves checking for and interpreting any changes in land areas on or near borders (such as beaten-down grass or brush) that indicate many people are traveling over them.

Border agents continually inspect land borders on foot, on horseback, or in motorized vehicles for signs the borders are being breached. Aiding the patrol in its mission are about 650 miles (1,046 km) of fences, walls, and other obstructions along parts of the border with Mexico to make border crossings difficult. However, agents must continually inspect the human-made obstacles because they are frequently breached. The Border Patrol also employs a fleet of 109 vessels to guard US borders in coastal waters as well as those around Puerto Rico, a US territory, and in lakes, rivers, and other waterways linking the United States and Canada. Agents in the patrol's Tunnel Entry team also locate and search underground tunnels used to smuggle illegal immigrants and materials across the border.

How Do You Become a Border Patrol Agent?

Education

Border Patrol agents generally need a college degree in a field related to law enforcement or criminal justice. However, some postsecondary education and various types of qualifying work experience such as other law enforcement background or military service may be helpful. The study of Spanish is also important because many illegal immigrants come from Spanish-speaking countries.

Certification and Licensing

Applicants must pass the three-part US Customs and Border Protection Border Patrol entrance examination. The first part tests logical reasoning skills. The second tests whether candidates speak Spanish or, for non-Spanish speakers, their ability to learn a foreign language. The third assesses the applicant's job-related experiences and achievements. Applicants who are accepted must pass a nineteen-week training course at the Border Patrol Academy in Artesia, New Mexico. The course includes instruction in immigration law, law enforcement and firearms training, physical conditioning, and driving skills so candidates can operate vehicles safely. Applicants who do not speak Spanish will be taught the language.

Volunteer Work and Internships

US Customs and Border Protection, a law enforcement agency that includes the Border Patrol, has internship programs for high school students and recent college graduates. The internships may include a wide variety of activities, such as field trips to border patrol areas. Interns may also be involved in helping process passengers and control crowds at airports and seaports, observing and assisting surveillance operations, and observing searches of vessels. Some of the internships are paid.

Skills and Personality

Being in good physical condition is just one of the many attributes borders agents need. Knowing how to use firearms and speak Spanish is helpful, but applicants can learn those skills in training at the Border Patrol Academy. Agents need good verbal and written communications skills to write reports and interact with the public and other law enforcement personnel. They need to be able to get along with many different types of people and work well with others as part of a team. Agents must be able to remain calm under stressful conditions, including situations involving personal danger. They must also have problem-solving skills and be able to exercise good judgment in deciding how to handle new or unexpected situations. Agents need to speak Spanish or learn to speak it, because so many people who try to illegally enter the United States are from Spanish-speaking countries.

Bravery and compassion are two other characteristics that many Border Patrol agents possess. Many of the illegal immigrants who try to cross into the United States get into dangerous situations. In July 2016 Justin Mitchell, an agent in the Border Patrol's Laredo, Texas, area, helped save four illegal border crossers who were drowning in the Rio Grande. The river marks part of the border between Texas and Mexico. In a *Laredo Morning Times* newspaper story, Mario Martinez, Mitchell's boss, said the river is dangerous for anyone, and "I commend him for risking his life to save others."

On the Job

Employers

The US Border Patrol is a federal law enforcement agency within the US Department of Homeland Security.

Working Conditions

There is no typical day for Border Patrol agents. But on April 21, 2016, the *Texas Tribune* newspaper website featured nine photographs showing the range of things a group of agents did one day while patrolling the Rio Grande near Roma, Texas. One picture shows two agents searching the riverbank for five people reported to have crossed into the United States on a raft. A second photo shows agents inspecting 313 pounds (142 kg) of marijuana they seized after chasing away smugglers who had used rafts to carry it across the river into US territory. Other pictures show footprints in sand and discarded clothing, clues that illegal immigrants or criminals had passed through the area.

The nation's southern border is its most vulnerable because it is so long and so many people from Mexico and Central America cross it to enter the country. But agents must also patrol the border with Canada thousands of miles north for illegal activity on both land and water. Lake Ontario forms a watery border between Canada and the United States. In a 2014 interview with WROC, a Rochester, New

A Border Patrol agent talks with an undocumented immigrant apprehended near the Texas-Mexico border. These agents monitor the US borders in an effort to prevent illegal entry.

York, television station, Agent Miki Ahl explained one method she uses to spot illegal lake border crossings. Ahl said she watches for boats that have their lights off coming ashore in the middle of the night because "that's something that is not a typical thing that you would be seeing."

The vast geographical scope of Border Patrol activity reflects an important condition of the job—agents must be willing to accept assignments anywhere along the nation's borders. Agents also have to be willing to work rotating shifts, which can interfere with sleep and private lives. They sometimes have to work shifts longer than eight hours or during weekends and holidays.

Guarding the border itself is only one of many tasks agents have. On May 9, 2016, agents went to a home in Edinburg, Texas, and found thirty-five illegal immigrants, including three juveniles from Mexico and Honduras. They took the immigrants into custody and arrested a US citizen and a Mexican national holding the people. The agency worked with other law enforcement agencies to find the illegal immigrants and make the arrests. It is common for agents to cooperate with other law enforcement officers in keeping the border secure.

Physical discomfort and danger from the elements are an ever-present concern—both for agents and for the people who illegally cross into the United States. For example, agents working outdoors sometimes have to endure extreme weather ranging from desert heat to freezing cold. In early June 2016 the Border Patrol briefly put its Search, Trauma, and Rescue unit on high alert because temperatures in parts of Arizona were predicted to hit 117°F (47°C). The unit provides emergency aid to agents, illegal immigrants, civilians, and even smugglers who are stricken by the heat. In a *Casa Grande (Arizona) Dispatch* newspaper story, Chief Patrol Agent Anthony J. Porvaznik said agents were equally committed to "reducing heat-related injuries and preventing deaths" of anyone they encounter while on patrol. And they frequently do encounter desperate people, including mothers with children, who try to cross deserts in the US Southwest without adequate water or food. Some of these individuals were abandoned by smugglers who dropped them off and sent them on their way alone. Others are simply following directions they received from others who have made the journey north.

Agents also sometimes have dangerous confrontations with armed smugglers. In December 2010 agent Brian Terry was shot to death near the border with Mexico near Rio Rico, Arizona, when he and three other agents had a shoot-out with criminals looking for drug smugglers to rob. For protection, agents wear body armor and are heavily armed. But in 2016 some agents were requesting even more sophisticated equipment like night vision goggles, as well as more agents, to improve their safety. Despite the sometimes difficult or hazardous working conditions, most agents like the work they do, says Chris Cabrera, an agent who works in the Rio Grande valley sector of the Border Patrol. In a May 31, 2016, newspaper story in the *Brownsville (Texas) Herald*, Cabrera said, "Overall people in the [Rio Grande] sector love their job."

One reason that some agents love this work is they can do it on horseback. Shawn Rodgers is a member of the Nogales, Arizona,

Station Horse Patrol Unit. In an August 19, 2016, story in the *Arizona Daily Star*, Rodgers said agents on horses travel quickly to trouble spots. And Rodgers said when agents yell "Dónde vas? Tenemos caballos" ("Where are you going? We have horses") at people they are chasing, those people know they are being pursued on horseback and cannot escape arrest.

Earnings

The median pay for a Border Patrol agent in 2016 was $64,000. Starting pay for new agents ranges from $32,318 to $48,968, depending on education and work experience, including time spent in law enforcement. Agents at the high end of the pay scale earn $93,470. Agents also receive paid vacation time and health care.

Opportunities for Advancement

Agents can advance through seniority, positive job reviews, and promotions; those who perform well have opportunities for promotion to higher-level positions such as overseeing other agents. They can transfer to other areas or types of work within the agency that require more skill or additional college education than their current positions.

What Is the Future Outlook for Border Patrol Agents?

The number of Border Patrol agents nearly doubled from eleven thousand to twenty thousand after 2001. In 2016 the Bureau of Labor Statistics predicted a 4 percent increase in the number of agent jobs through 2024. Ongoing concerns about terrorist threats and illegal immigration could lead to a greater number of new agent positions in the future.

Find Out More

BorderPatrolEdu.org
website: www.borderpatroledu.org

This site has information on job requirements, salary, and education and training programs for those who want to pursue a career as a Border Patrol agent. It also features information about specific jobs and career paths.

National Border Patrol Council (NBPC)
website: www.bpunion.org

This is the union that represents eighteen thousand Border Patrol agents and support personnel. The site includes news and information on issues concerning the Border Patrol, its agents, and other employees.

US Customs and Border Protection (CBP)
website: www.cbp.gov/careers

The official website of the CBP, which is an agency of the Department of Homeland Security, features information about becoming a Border Patrol agent and other jobs within CBP. It also has links to information about programs for high school and college students.

Fish and Game Warden

At a Glance:
Fish and Game Warden

Minimum Educational Requirements

High school diploma or equivalent; some states require some college credits or a college degree

Personal Qualities

Good judgement of people, solid problem-solving skills, good at writing and oral communication

Certification and Licensing

Must pass game warden or police academy training

Working Conditions

Mostly outdoors in rugged terrain and all types of weather

Salary Range

Median annual salary of $52,780 in 2015

Number of Jobs

About 5,630 in 2015; of those, 5,100 with state governments

Future Job Outlook

A 2 percent job growth through 2024

What Does a Fish and Game Warden Do?

Fish and game wardens (sometimes called wildlife officers or other titles) protect and conserve the nation's lands and waterways and the animals, birds, and fish that inhabit them. These individuals have the same powers as their law enforcement counterparts patrolling urban and suburban areas, highways, and waterways. They carry and use firearms, investigate law violations, interview and arrest suspects, and testify in court cases. Wardens can also search homes and vehicles for evidence of illegal trapping or killing of wildlife.

Wardens enforce fishing, hunting, and boating regulations as well as environmental laws that prohibit the illegal dumping of hazardous waste. Some wardens even enforce laws on seas bordering their states. Connecticut wardens, for example, help regulate commercial harvesting of fish and shellfish in the Atlantic Ocean. In states bordered by oceans, wardens sometimes team with the US Coast Guard to work law enforcement situations. Wardens in every state also cooperate with local, state, and federal law enforcement agencies to investigate crimes in outdoor areas or catch criminals hiding in them. Wardens also work with the US Department of Homeland Security on incidents involving terrorism or illegal immigration.

Wardens perform many important tasks besides law enforcement. They prepare and issue legal documents like hunting and fishing licenses and register deer or other wildlife taken legally by hunters. Wardens protect the tens of millions of people who engage in a wide variety of outdoor sports and recreational activities. They instruct the general public about hunting, boating, and outdoor safety. They police public outdoor areas to make sure people obey boating, hunting, and motor vehicle laws so they will not harm themselves or others. Wardens conduct search-and-rescue operations for lost or injured people. Wardens even help manage natural resources used for hunting, fishing, and other recreational purposes. For example, they often participate in biological studies of animal and fish habitats to track growing or diminishing populations of certain species.

Those tasks all have one goal—to protect an area's wildlife and natural beauty. Grahame Jones is a Texas Parks & Wildlife law enforcement specialist. In a 2013 story in the *Houston Chronicle*, Jones said he works to prevent "the loss of many of our state treasures" from illegal hunting and fishing so future generations can continue to enjoy the state's wildlife resources.

How Do You Become a Fish and Game Warden?

Education

Some states require applicants to at least have a high school diploma or equivalent, while others require a minimum of an associate's degree. Still other states, Texas and Montana among them, require a bachelor's degree in wildlife management, zoology, police science, law enforcement, biology, environmental science, or animal science. Candidates with minimal college work may be accepted if they have experience in the military or law enforcement.

Certification and Licensing

Applicants undergo a warden or police training program that teaches them about the laws they will enforce and the basics of policing such as investigating crimes and subduing suspects. The training period varies from state to state, but in Texas, for instance, the initial training period is fifteen weeks; additional training is given as needed in the future. Applicants are also taught how to patrol their assigned areas to spot law violations, how to search for people lost in wilderness areas, and how to rescue people from dangerous situations like drowning. They also learn how to use firearms and have to pass a test in their use to become a warden. Applicants must also pass a test for physical strength and endurance that, in some states, includes being able to swim. Candidates are also tested for skills like written communication, reading and comprehension, reasoning and analytical ability, and problem solving.

Volunteer Work and Internships

The federal government and many states have internships for high school and college students. Some internship positions are paid and some are not. Montana's warden internship program is a short-term work experience for college students. Wisconsin's internship program is an on-the-job training experience like an apprenticeship open to high school and college students. Such programs provide opportunities to gain experience in the field by working with wardens.

Skills and Personality

Wardens work outdoors most of the time. A love and appreciation of natural settings and personal experience in wilderness areas and activities like hiking, camping, and hunting will make it easier for candidates to do and enjoy this job. Wardens often work alone. Thus, they must be able to handle various situations by themselves, from arresting law breakers to rescuing someone whose life is in danger. And wardens know anything can happen. On August 16, 2016, a warden discovered a 4-foot (1.2-m) alligator sunning himself on a rock in a creek in Fremont, California. Officials believe someone abandoned the alligator when it got too big to keep. Because it posed a danger to the public, the warden shot the alligator. Solid critical-thinking and problem-solving skills, decisiveness, and good judgment are also necessary to do this job. Additional requirements for this job include good written and oral communication skills and the ability to listen attentively and understand what people are telling them. Wardens also need to be able to judge the character of people they encounter in the course of their workday.

On the Job

Employers

The US Fish & Wildlife Service employs agents to enforce laws on recreational use and environmental protection of federal lands and wildlife resources. State and some local governments also hire fish and game wardens for similar duties in the areas under their jurisdiction.

Working Conditions

Fish and game wardens spend most of their time patrolling large areas that can include rugged and hazardous terrain. Depending on where they work, they may patrol on foot; in trucks, snowmobiles, boats, and planes; or even on horseback. They work outdoors in all types of weather from desert heat to bitter cold and even dangerous conditions like floods, tornadoes, and blizzards. Working hours can include evenings, weekends, and holidays. Night shifts can be hard on a warden's personal life. But Erin Crossman, a Connecticut Environmental Conservation Police officer, likes the challenge of that shift. In a 2013 *Outdoor Life* magazine story, Crossman said it is "the most exciting and interesting time to be on patrol" because she is so busy responding to calls about illegal hunting practices such as shining a light on a deer so that it will freeze and be easier to shoot. Crossman is also busy at night because she is a K9 officer. Other law enforcement agencies often ask her and her dog, Ellie, to help with tracking a lost person or suspected criminal. Wardens also work longer and harder during peak times like hunting and fishing seasons, when more people flock to their areas.

There is no typical day for fish and game wardens, because they have a wide variety of duties. Although wardens often work alone, they have a lot of contact with the public. During hunting and fishing seasons, they may check to make sure people have proper licenses and have not violated laws by taking more fish or game than regulations allow. Wardens may visit schools or private groups to educate them about the environment or hunting. They may help biologists or ecologists gather data on wildlife habitats and populations or water quality to assess programs to preserve them and the environment.

The job of wardens can vary from day to day because they employ many different, sometimes unusual tools and tactics to perform their duties. Vermont game wardens use robotic deer to catch poachers hunting out of season. The Washington Department of Fish & Wildlife uses six Karelian bear dogs for wildlife research, for law enforcement, and to condition bears, cougars, and moose to avoid humans. This Finnish breed of dog is also a goodwill ambassador for the department because the dogs are so lovable and gentle that small kids love to pet them. Texas game wardens are among many law enforcement officials using the Internet to track down illegal sales related to exotic species such as leopard pelts or endangered species like the Texas tortoise.

A major task wardens perform is to rescue and save the lives of people who encounter trouble outdoors. An example of that occurred on February 22, 2016, when Wisconsin warden Dale Hochhausen saved the life of an ice fisher who had fallen through thin ice on the Mississippi River in Stoddard, Wisconsin. A Department of Natural Resources story said Hochhausen saw a man identified as Harold fall through the ice. Hochhausen edged out on the ice and was able to pull the man to safety by grabbing his parka. As in everything wardens do, Hochhausen filed a report on his heroic action. One of the less exciting tasks wardens have is to maintain daily logs on their activities and write reports on arrests and other incidents. Paperwork is mostly done electronically, either in the field or the office.

Like all law enforcement officers, fish and game wardens know their jobs can be dangerous, especially because so many people they meet while doing their jobs are armed. Jonathan Parker is a Maine game warden. In a story in the Maine newspaper the *Irregular*, he admitted, "The potential for danger is always there. You never know who you are dealing with. You never know what is going to happen." An example of that danger was the shooting death on March 17, 2007, of Texas game warden Justin Hurst. He was shot on his thirty-fourth birthday while trying to arrest a man suspected of illegally hunting at night.

The job of a warden can be rewarding as well as difficult and dangerous. Terry Grosz is a retired warden who worked for both the California and US Fish & Wildlife Service. In an interview in 2016 with Chicago radio station WBEZ, Grosz said being a warden is a worthwhile career because wardens protect something valuable. Said Grosz, "Wildlife dies without making a sound. So the only voice it's got is yours."

Earnings

In 2015 the median annual wage for fish and game wardens was $52,780, with the lowest 10 percent earning $34,620 and the highest 10 percent $76,510.

Opportunities for Advancement

As fish and game wardens gain more experience, they advance in rank. They may also move to jobs with other law enforcement agencies that may be more rewarding financially.

What Is the Future Outlook for Fish and Game Wardens?

The number of fish and game wardens will grow by 2 percent through 2024, which is less than the average for all occupations. But for a person who has a passion for the outdoors and likes the idea of combining that passion with a job in law enforcement, this could be a career worth pursuing.

Find Out More

GameWardenEDU.org
website: www.gamewardenedu.org

This site has information on job requirements, salary, and education and training programs for those who want to pursue a career as a game warden. It also features information about specific jobs and career paths.

GameWarden.org
website: www.gamewarden.org

This site has information on education, work conditions, and other aspects of the career of a fish and game warden. It also provides links to fish and game warden jobs by state.

US Fish & Wildlife Service
website: www.fws.gov

This website features career information for federal jobs in this field. It also has details about student internships and youth volunteer programs.

Animal Control Officer

At a Glance:
Animal Control Officer

Minimum Educational Requirements
A high school diploma or equivalent

Personal Qualities
An affinity for many types of animals, decisive, compassionate, able to work with people who may be emotional or angry

Certification and Licensing
Required by some employers

Working Conditions
A lot of driving and visits to locations; some office work

Salary Range
Mean annual salary of $35,330 in 2015

Number of Jobs
About 13,180 in 2015; of those, 11,840 with government agencies

Future Job Outlook
An 11 percent job growth through 2024

What Does an Animal Control Officer Do?

When people think of animal control, they often picture someone in a truck scooping up and impounding stray dogs. That is part of the job of an animal control officer, but there is much more to it than that. Hilary Cohen is an animal control officer in Norfolk, Massachusetts. This is how Cohen described her job in a 2016 *MetroWest Daily News* story: "In a nutshell, I help people that have animal problems, and animals that have people problems." On June 16, 2016, Cohen posted a picture of two black goats on the Norfolk, Massachusetts, Animal Control and Shelter Facebook page. Cohen said they appeared to be lost and asked if anyone knew their owner. The problem was resolved in just two hours when

An animal control officer brings two small dogs to a shelter. Animal control officers respond to emergencies and investigate reports of abandoned and abused or neglected animals.

Cohen received a reply from someone who knew their owners.

Animal control officers—sometimes called dog wardens, dog-catchers, humane officers, and even animal cops—enforce laws and regulations involving animal welfare. Whatever their title, they patrol public areas, respond to emergency calls, and investigate reports of abandoned or lost animals and animals that are being mistreated. They deal with animals in a variety of situations, from saving injured or sick animals to capturing or killing those that are dangerous. Officers encounter household pets like dogs and cats, deer and other wildlife, and even exotic creatures like boa constrictors.

One of their most important jobs is to investigate complaints of animal abuse or neglect. An example is a person who has so many cats or dogs that the individual cannot properly care for them. Officers who find animals living in unsanitary or dangerous situations can remove them so they will not be harmed. Officers also investigate complaints of abuse such as people mistreating animals or using them in illegal fighting matches. Shirley Zindler wrote *The Secret Life of Dog Catchers*, a book about her work as a California animal control officer. In an interview on the Books & Bark website, she admitted, "I have my days where I can hardly bear the sadness and hurt that people wreak on their fellow people and animals." But Zindler said the emotional pain is worth it because "I feel like I'm making a difference."

Licensing animals and educating the public are two other duties of animal control officers. They make sure citizens properly license animals. For example, officers investigate reports of people owning exotic animals like lions or alligators that are prohibited by law because they pose a threat to public safety. Officers educate the public on how to properly care for animals, the differences between various types of animals, and laws regarding animals.

How Do You Become an Animal Control Officer?

Education

The minimum education requirement for animal control officers is a high school degree or equivalent. Some employers, however, require a college degree in animal science, veterinary science, or law enforcement. Applicants with a degree or at least some college credits usually have a greater chance of being hired. Employers may require applicants to undergo training for the job before hiring them. Once they are hired, officers may have to undergo additional training to stay current with laws and new knowledge and techniques on how to handle animals and different situations involving them.

Certification and Licensing

Some states require applicants to pass an examination to be certified. The examination tests their knowledge about how to capture animals, recognize animal disease, and act in situations such as animal abuse or animals endangering the lives of people.

Volunteer Work and Internships

One way to get experience for a job as an animal control officer is to do volunteer work at an animal shelter, humane society, or other organization that cares for or promotes animal welfare.

Skills and Personality

Animal control officers should be knowledgeable about animals and passionate about how they are treated. But they also need good people skills, whether it is to show sympathy for people whose pets have died or to defuse a tense situation. Many interactions with the public can be emotional, such as when officers warn people to always walk their dog on a leash. Some situations can become hostile and lead to violence when officers remove pets that have bitten someone or take animals from people keeping so many pets that they cannot properly care for them. When officers interact with people suspected of abusing animals, they must control their personal emotions about the mistreatment so they can deal fairly with them. Officers often work alone, so they must be self-reliant and able to make good decisions.

On the Job

Employers

Local, state, and federal government agencies employ animal control officers. Not all local governments have full-time officers. Instead, some police departments and other law enforcement agencies allow a member of their force to handle those duties part time. In addition, private organizations like the Humane Society and the American Society for the Prevention of Cruelty to Animals and some for-profit businesses employ people who perform duties similar to those of animal control officers.

Working Conditions

Animal control officers sometimes work in an office setting answering calls about injured, abused, or dangerous animals and writing reports about what they have done that day. But they spend most of their time in the field, and their "office" is the service truck or van they use to respond to reports concerning animals. Those vehicles have cages to safely transport animals to shelters or, when necessary, animal hospitals for medical treatment. Officers patrol urban, suburban, and even wilderness areas in national parks to spot problems or potential problems involving animals. When officers make arrests or charge people with violations of laws concerning animals, they collect evidence of abuse or neglect so offenders can be prosecuted. They testify in court when those cases go to trial. Working hours may include night and weekend hours and holidays.

There is no typical day for animal control officers, because they deal with many different situations. They respond to reports of deer or other wild animals venturing into urban areas, animals run over by cars, a rabid skunk that could bite and infect people, bats that get into a home, or even a wild turkey that killed itself by flying into the window of a home. Manchester, Connecticut, animal control officer Elease McConnell handled the call about the turkey, but most of her work involves controlling dogs that run loose, bite people, or cause problems in other ways. In a 2016 story about her job in the *Hartford Courant* newspaper, McConnell stated, "There's a lot of happy endings." One was reuniting a Manchester man with his dog Lulu after she jumped out of his truck and ran off. But this job can also be emotionally draining. On the same day McConnell found Lulu, she learned that an abandoned dog she had taken to the Manchester animal shelter had to be put down because it was infected with parvovirus, a contagious disease deadly to dogs.

Animal control officers encounter aggressive animals that pose a risk to human safety. One such incident occurred in Ohio's Butler County in 2014 when a woman died after being attacked by a dog that was a family pet. Sheriff Richard K. Jones, who served as the county's dog warden, investigated the attack. In a sheriff's department news release, he said, "These type of tragedies are happening way too often, family pet or not." The dog was euthanized.

Animal control officers sometimes have to deal with a negative public image of their profession. It stems partly from the stereotype of villainous dogcatchers depicted in films like Disney's *Lady and the Tramp*. People may also dislike animal control officers because they fear officers will take away their pets if they have not registered them or are not properly caring for them. Darrell Hudson, a veteran animal officer in Memphis, Tennessee, said in a 2015 story in the *Commercial Appeal* newspaper that the negative public image is misguided. "We work with the citizens to get their animals back if they can get them back," Hudson said. "Every one of us on this job loves animals and want what's best for them. That's why we took the job. We love animals."

Animal control officers sometimes encounter threats from humans. Hudson's comments appeared in a story about bulletproof vests Memphis bought for its twenty animal control officers. They needed them for protection because some officers had been threatened by people with guns and even shot at while doing their job. In one case in 2012 in Sacramento, California, animal control officer Roy Curtis Marcum was gathering pets owned by Joseph Francis Corey after Corey had been served an eviction notice. Corey was still in the house, and he shot and killed Marcum. Corey was found guilty of first-degree murder.

Vicious or wild animals also pose a risk to officers. Esteban Rodriguez is an animal control officer in Dallas, Texas. In a 2016 *Dallas Morning News* story, Rodriguez talked about using a pole with a snare on one end to capture an aggressive dog. "Luckily, I was able to rope him with my catchpole. It was a one-shot thing. If I had missed, I probably would have gotten bit," Rodriguez says. Officers' health may also be at risk if they come into contact with diseased animals.

But animal control officers also have more enjoyable tasks, like lecturing at schools about how to care for animals and giving tips on what not to do in situations involving larger, more dangerous animals. Sherry DeGenova is a veteran animal control officer in Hartford, Connecticut. One of the best parts of her job is when someone adopts a dog, cat, or other stray or abandoned animal from the Hartford Animal Shelter. In a 2015 *Hartford Courant* newspaper story, DeGenova said, "Any animal that I adopt out after its time here is an accomplishment in this job."

Earnings

Animal control officers in 2015 had a median salary of $33,450, meaning that half the workers in this career make more and half make less. Pay in 2015 for the bottom 10 percent was $20,830 and for the top 10 percent $53,190. However, almost all animal control officers are government employees who generally have lower pay but better pensions and benefits than similar workers in the private sector.

Opportunities for Advancement

Animal control officers can advance to supervisory or management positions in the government agency or organization that employs them. Animal control officers can use their knowledge and work experience to get jobs with private organizations and businesses that work with animals. With further education, officers can switch careers by going into other law enforcement work or animal-related careers like veterinary medicine.

What Is the Future Outlook for Animal Control Officer?

The need for animal control officers is growing. In 2015 there were 13,180 animal control jobs, including 11,840 with government agencies. Such jobs are expected to increase by 11 percent through 2024, nearly twice as fast as the predicted 6.5 percent growth for all jobs.

Find Out More

The Humane Society of the United States
website: www.humanesociety.org

This is the nation's largest and most effective animal protection organization. The section on the organization's work features information about animal rescue and care, animal advocacy, and shelters. This site is a good resource for anyone considering a career as an animal control officer.

National Animal Care & Control Association (NACA)
website: www.nacanet.org

This site has information on training for this career, news articles about this job, and resources for animal control officers. NACA also certifies people for this field.

State Humane Association of California
website: www.californiastatehumane.org

Although this website includes specific information about jobs in California, it also has a large amount of general information for people interested in this career regardless of the state they want work in.

Interview with an FBI Special Agent

Peter James Jurack joined the FBI as a special agent in 2002. In 2016 he was a supervisor special agent in Washington, DC, in charge of a squad that deals with violent crime. When Jurack first approached the FBI about a job, he was in his twenties (the average age of FBI recruits is thirty-one), had a political science degree, and had some job experience but not in law enforcement. The author interviewed Jurack by telephone.

Q: How did you become interested in a career in the FBI?

A: I can think back to playing cops and robbers with my brothers. I always seemed to be the cop. I always had an eye toward law enforcement. The FBI recruiter said, "You're a little young and need some experience, go be a cop." I spent four and a half years with the Virginia Beach [Virginia] police department as a uniformed officer, undercover officer for a while, and detective. I think that law enforcement experience was tremendously beneficial for me, especially the time I was working in narcotics doing seizures of drugs.

Q: What finally helped motivate you to join the FBI?

A: I was a post-9/11 hire. There was a surge of patriotism at the time, of a sense, a need, to give back to your country. I think that was a huge part of it. I was a Boy Scout and Eagle Scout and the sense of commitment to country and service was ingrained in me. There is a sense of duty to country and commitment [in working for the FBI] because you don't do it to become rich.

Q: How was working for the FBI different than being a police officer?

A: I think it was very plain in Virginia Beach we were focused on small-time drug dealers. But when we [the FBI] started working against the drug cartels in Chicago we had a nationwide focus that came from a completely different scope in terms of organization [from going after] street dealers to wholesale distributors. Our reach was down into Mexico and beyond. This was very rewarding work for my first year in the bureau [when] you are running major operations and taking out major players in the cartel. You can see a difference you're making by doing that.

Q: Is working for the FBI as glamorous as movies and television make it appear?

A: It's 90 percent routine followed by 10 percent hair on fire, of extreme activity, of adrenaline rush. We may go through a period of time when there is not a lot of activity but then you are chasing someone responsible for eight or ten bank robberies. [People] may see the glamour of the job in making an arrest but there is a lot of work that comes after that. There is a lot of paperwork, a lot of work and planning behind the scenes to put a case together against an individual.

Q: What do you like about the job?

A: For me I think as a [supervisor] I enjoy being a leader [and] the sense of camaraderie is tremendous, the satisfaction of working with other individuals toward a common goal. The most satisfying part of my job is serving as a mentor to younger agents. And it is also satisfying to send a violent criminal away for a long sentence.

Q: What do you dislike about the job?

A: I think the administrative side, there are some things that can become tedious like filing reports and filling out forms. But you accept it as part of the job you do. Sometimes the thing that can be the most difficult is when you might see squabbles between different agencies. . . . Sometimes locals don't want to give up a case that should be federal. That can get a little tedious.

Q: What personal quality do you find most valuable for this type of work?

A: I think for high school students if they are looking toward this career your personal integrity is probably the single most important quality. That is going to tell more about you than anything else because it affects the decisions you make. Your life experiences and the decisions you make will affect you later in life. Approach everything in life like it is a tryout for the future.

Q: How should young people prepare for an FBI career?

A: I would tell them to have a very diverse background, never pigeon-hole themselves in one area. The bureau doesn't hire one category of people. I think being well rounded is the most important thing. . . . Being active in athletics, student government, and other outside activities is incredibly important.

Other Jobs in Law Enforcement

Accident investigator
Alcohol, Tobacco, and Firearms
  agent
Arson investigator
Civilian intelligence agent
Computer forensics expert
Counterterrorism expert
Cybersecurity worker
Deportation officer
Deputy sheriff
Diplomatic security agent
Drug Enforcement
  Administration agent
Fingerprint technician
Firearms technician
Fire investigator
Forensic photographer
Fraud investigator
Gaming surveillance officer
Handwriting examiner
Immigration and Customs
  Enforcement agent

Intelligence analyst
Internal Revenue Service special
  agent
K9 police officer
Legal investigator
Medical examiner
Military police officer
Motorcycle officer
National Security Agency officer
Postal inspector
Private detective
Probation officer
Psychological profiler
Secret Service agent
Security guard
State Patrol Officer
State Trooper
Surveillance specialist
Transit and railroad police
  officer
Transportation security screener
US marshal

Editor's Note: The US Department of Labor's Bureau of Labor Statistics provides information about hundreds of occupations. The agency's *Occupational Outlook Handbook* describes what these jobs entail, the work environment, education and skill requirements, pay, future outlook, and more. The *Occupational Outlook Handbook* may be accessed online at www.bls.gov/ooh.

Index

Picture Credits

About the Author

Michael V. Uschan has written ninety-nine books, including *Life of an American Soldier in Iraq*, for which he won the 2005 Council for Wisconsin Writers Juvenile Nonfiction Award. It was the second time he won the award. Uschan began his career as a writer and editor with United Press International, a wire service that provided stories to newspapers, radio, and television. He and his wife, Barbara, reside in the Milwaukee suburb of Franklin, Wisconsin.